Boundaries In Marriage

Line Between Right And Wrong

2nd Edition

Jeffery Dawson

within this book without the consent of the author or copyright owner. Legal action will be pursued if this is breached.

Disclaimer Notice:

Please note the information contained within this document is for educational and entertainment purposes only. Every attempt has been made to provide accurate, up to date and reliable complete information. No warranties of any kind are expressed or implied. Readers acknowledge that the author is not engaging in the rendering of legal, financial, medical or professional advice.

By reading this document, the reader agrees that under no circumstances are we responsible for any losses, direct or indirect, which are incurred as a result of the use of information contained within this document, including, but not limited to, —errors, omissions, or inaccuracies.

Table of Contents

Introduction

If you have ever wondered what should come between a man and his wife then you would be wrong to think that these are people who should have no boundaries. Boundaries are the distances that people place between themselves and others, though healthy boundaries exist even in the most intimate and close relationships. These are brought about by mutual respect for one another and are not negative at all. In fact, they positively reinforce the importance of each person within that relationship.

This book explains to people thinking of getting married, or those who are experiencing difficulty within their marriage, how boundaries should be set up for the mutual benefit of both parties. These strengthen a marriage and make it much more lasting. In cases cited within the book, you will notice that the end result of imposing acceptable boundaries is that couples are able to find a harmony that works well and that they do not have unreasonable expectations of each other. When this happens, then the relationship can be stronger.

Boundaries apply in both directions. They are not unreasonable expectations, but well thought out expectations that come about from a mutual accord. This book will guide you through the complexity of male/female boundaries so that you are able to understand your marriage better and find more happiness and contentment in that union. If you are experiencing difficulty within your marriage, chances are that boundaries will be the culprit. Setting boundaries that are acceptable to both of you may help you to get the marriage back on course.

If, however, you are starting out in a new marriage and are looking forward to making your promises to each other, this is a great time to understand what boundaries within a marriage are all about, so that you can set off on the right footing and help make your marriage a success. With this book as your guide, you will be able to make decisions together, based on your hopes, wishes and ambitions that will help you and your partner to understand each other's needs from the moment that you utter the words "I do."

Chapter 1 – The Unhappy Couple

When couples experience unhappiness, it stems from misunderstanding. A woman may, for example, nag her husband because she feels that his behavior shows lack of respect for her. She doesn't feel loved and therefore puts more expectations on the shoulders of her husband to compensate for not feeling loved. She needs more concrete proof that her husband cares about her and thus her nagging is her way of demanding attention. He, in turn, feels that her nagging makes her a miserable person to be with and the vicious circle of discontentment begins. No one wins in a situation such as this, and it's common for marriage counselors to experience this kind of lack of rapport between couples.

Where couples need to take responsibility and understand boundaries is in their personal feelings. In the instance shown above, the woman feels unloved. Perhaps the way she is presenting herself to her husband doesn't really make her very lovable. Instead of breaking into her husband's personal space and demanding he change his attitude, perhaps what she needs to recognize is that she herself has boundary problems. She needs to keep her feelings in check and is the only person responsible for the negative feelings that she is experiencing. Thus, she should not use these as an excuse to expect her husband to change. Examining the relationship and looking at why her husband is unhappy would be much more fruitful. The man in the above scenario begins to see his wife as imposing herself upon his boundaries, though clearly, there is something wrong with his communication skills if his wife feels unloved. He needs to learn to express that love in a more tangible way. Once he does, what he finds happens is that she begins to appreciate him more. Shouting at her when she nags is not the answer to the problem and will make the matter worse. Looking at the boundaries of his own behavior toward her, he is able to work out ways that are more demonstrable of his love.

The problem is that when two people live together, they often make the mistake of seeing themselves as extensions of each other. In reality, they are still two separate people, but they are living within a given space, each one independent and each with individual needs. The sooner you drop the idea that you are an extension of someone else, the healthier your attitude will become. You cannot be responsible for your partner's attitudes, his likes, his dislikes and the friends that he chooses to make, without crossing a boundary and that's not fair.

Similarly, he can't have those expectations of you. What you can do is work together to make your differences complement each other. She wants to go to night classes. He doesn't usually babysit. Thus, she feels he is being unreasonable. In order to get a marriage to work well, you need to work together to find a system that gives equal respect to both parties. For example, a man should never stop his wife from doing something that she wants to do, simply because he expects her to be at home cooking dinner. A woman should not expect her husband to give up his friends because she wants him exclusively to herself. The boundaries need to be defined so that each is able to live his/her life within set boundaries that work for the marriage as well as for their own personal needs.

Try and think of boundaries a little like a garden fence. It isn't constructed so that you can dictate to a neighbor how he behaves on his side of the fence. Similarly, boundaries between a couple are not placed as an obstacle. They are placed within the marriage to protect it from harm. If you feel that something is wrong within your marriage, the first place to look to see if the boundaries are set correctly is at yourself, rather than at your partner. Those who look at the partner as being the sole reason for problems are not looking hard enough at their own expectations, which may be unreasonable, and crossing the boundaries of respect.

People who don't understand boundaries within a relationship will not be able to listen to their partner with any objectivity. Therefore, when bad experiences occur, they are not able to help because they are too interdependent upon the relationship and are not sufficiently able to distance themselves from the problem without being defensive. The problem with looking at personal difficulties in this manner is that the party who is aggrieved will be less likely to discuss their problem if they know that the problem will be met with a defensive answer.

A man who has problems with his sexual performance may find himself criticized by a wife who feels he no longer loves her. This helps no one at all. If, however, she is able to empathize, she may be able to help him through the problem and see the relationship go back to normal once his problem is solved. The point is that boundaries need to be drawn which gives each party the right to discuss things with their partner without feeling that they have to justify what they are saying or placate their partner because they don't feel the same way. Forget the idea that couples are one entity. They never will be. They are two people with boundaries that make their lives happier and safer places to be. Remember, the main rule is that "it isn't about you." and you may find you can open a listening ear to your partner more readily than if you believe it is about you.

Chapter 2 – Personal Boundaries

Society has already imposed normal behavior patterns between women and men and just because a man and woman live under the same roof doesn't mean that these have to disappear. In fact, they become more exaggerated because you live every day within the same home. Women may have expectations of their man in that they expect a man to treat the home with respect. A man who throws his clothing onto the floor every night and expects his wife to pick it up is treating her badly because it isn't her responsibility to do that.

Similarly, a woman would not expect a man to iron her clothes or be present in the room when she is doing personal things. She may be embarrassed when he walks in on her while she is waxing her bikini line or even her mustache. These are unspoken boundaries of decency. A man would similarly not expect a woman to walk into the bathroom when he is sitting on the toilet.

There are certain boundaries, which come as natural to most people and these need to be upheld in a marriage, to show mutual respect for each other.

One woman who was married used to iron her husband's clothing and place it upon his chair. He was particularly fussy about where it was put within his closet, so she respected his wish and left it on the chair. He started to move it around from the chair to the floor and never get around to putting it away. In the end it was more creased than it would have been before she ironed it. Her way around this was to place his washing on one side and get him to iron it himself, stating that she didn't have time to iron things if they were merely going to be placed on the floor.

There were two ways that she could have behaved. She could have nagged him, but that would have made him very negative indeed. She chose simply to adjust what she was prepared to do for him until his response was a little more respectful. It worked. Within a week, he was tired of ironing and sent her a bunch of flowers with a note saying sorry.

Similarly, if a wife had prepared a meal for a set time and her husband was always late for his meals, she would be perfectly within her rights to place his meal in the microwave and get him to eat it warmed up, or to adjust the time of the meal so that it suited both of them, instead of nagging and getting upset about it.

The point is that the behavior of two people within the same family cannot be dictated by one person. It needs to be something that's decided upon by two people and then boundaries are used to keep them within acceptable parameters, once an agreement is made. You cannot adjust your husband's behavior. A man cannot adjust his wife's behavior, but by setting boundaries, which are acceptable to, both, either can discuss a change of those boundaries when time dictates that a change is necessary.

Relationships have boundaries for a purpose. Without them, people could do exactly what they want to do without regard for their partner. Since they are joined in holy matrimony, boundaries help the couple to set up a system of communication and behavior that works for everyone. A man and woman should know each other well enough to realize what reactions cause embarrassment and should respect that there comes a time when mutual respect is more important than making fun of someone and embarrassing them.

The acceptable behavioral boundaries between men and women will have already been established during the couple's courtship and their experience with peers. Thus, these should extend into a marriage so that mutual respect is not only to be expected but is to be a prime concern to both man and woman.

There are times when a man or woman can find himself or herself in a very vulnerable situation. A woman who is expected to cater for the boss, and who is inexperienced, may need help rather than being criticized and made to feel small. A man, having to deal with repairs in the home, may not actually be experienced in such repairs. A woman should make allowance for this and realize that it's not fair to put undue pressure on him to do something he is unfamiliar with. By using mutual respect, and setting aside behavior that embarrasses either party, the couple is indeed making boundaries that work for them. When they do, the marriage can run smoothly and both parties are equally happy with their lot.

Chapter 3 – 'Til Death Do Us Part

When you think of marriage in terms of a life sentence, it seems a very difficult situation to allow yourself to get into. Effectively, you promise your lifetime to one loved one and they, in return, make similar promises. You promise to love, honor and obey and also promise that you will be faithful to that person and you would be right to expect the same promises to apply equally to them. The problem is that many couples interpret the promises a little too broadly. They believe that there's a kind of ownership involved in marriage and that's one of the first things a couple needs to let go of. No one can own another human being. Here are some thoughts that you may have considered as being part of any marriage over a period of time:

1. Self-indulgence

2. Obedience to the point of letting go of personal liberty

3. Being obliged to serve your partner

4. Being obliged to behave in a set way that is thrown up as an expectation

Unfortunately, none of these make up a successful marriage. That's why boundaries exist. When love happens between two people who have self-respect and respect for each other, they free themselves from the above because love actually doesn't require someone else to act in a specific way. All that love wants is to continue to be a mutual emotion that is shared. Unfortunately, some people interpret this in different ways and that's where the boundaries become blurred.

One of the biggest issues that marriage counselors have to face is when a couple gets angry at each other and start to throw blame. Couples who argue tend to blame each other for what goes wrong in the marriage and that's the first place to look for solutions. The arguments may have started over small things, but eventually, the situation comes down to one party blaming the other for their own unhappiness. As stated in an earlier chapter, people do not become responsible for the happiness of another human being just because they are married. They are not an extension of that person and if something is making a marriage unhappy, then boundaries will have been crossed somewhere along the line.

If you find yourself asking, "Why won't he do what I want him to do?" you also need to ask yourself "Why would I expect him to be doing what I want him to do?" because at the end of the day, it's your own personal expectations which are making you unhappy. When you are unhappy and transfer negativity to him, he becomes less likely to be able to please you because he isn't able to get inside of your head to find out what made you unhappy in the first place. You cannot dictate how your partner will react, nor can you expect them to behave in a certain manner just because it's what you expect. Situations such as this arise when, for example, a woman overspends and a husband gets mad because they are always broke. A man may leave the house untidy and expect his wife to clean up after him.

When you restrict the freedom of another individual in any way, you cross boundaries. The wife who overspends may just be overspending because she doesn't know there isn't that much money in the bank. Open dialog will help to clear these problems out, rather than letting them brew and become so big that arguments ensue. If she wants more money, for example, what's to stop her getting a nice job that allows her that extra? If he doesn't want to clean up the house after himself, what's to stop her simply letting his mess build up and cleaning around it. He will soon get the message. The problem happens when the boundary is crossed that takes away individual choice and nagging occurs.

The aspects which are vital to a strong relationship are:

- Respect
- Responsibility
- Freedom

If you take any of these away from the marriage, you put up boundaries that are unacceptable. Without respect, a marriage won't last long. Without responsibility for self, the marriage may falter and without freedom, a marriage becomes a life sentence.

Thus, when setting boundaries, these should never restrict an individual to such an extent that the individual needs to change. In marriages, where a woman works toward changing her man, the boundaries are unreasonable and the same applies to a marriage, where a man has expectations that his woman will change. Acceptance, for better or for worse, is much healthier.

Chapter 4 – Where Boundaries Apply In A Marriage

Boundaries apply in different areas of a marriage and these don't depend upon the religion of the background of the couple. These depend upon decency, respect and thoughtfulness. The areas where these should apply would be the following areas:

- Responsibility

- Protection

- Feelings

- Attitudes and beliefs

- Personal values

- Choices

- Desires

- Spiritual needs

That may seem like a lot of ground to cover.

However, all of these affect the individual. Responsibility toward each other should have boundaries. A husband who takes responsibility for the finances and does not permit his wife to work may be overstepping the boundary of protection. She may wish to work and in insisting that she stays at home, he may be denying her the right to choice.

Protection is another area that should be covered by boundaries. How much protection is reasonable? How much is interfering? There have to be boundaries that are acceptable to both parties, and one cannot insist on protecting the other at the expense of their liberty.

Feelings and emotions do come into the picture. If you deliberately say things which you know will hurt feelings, then you overstep the emotional boundaries that should exist in a loving couple.

Personal values and beliefs are another area that is important. A woman who is Catholic, for example, may have strong religious conviction, while her husband may choose not to believe in God. However, each should respect the other's opinion, as this is something that cannot be dictated by another person.

Choices and desires are areas where people may come to loggerheads, although one must assume that if true love exists, it will make allowances for both to chase their dreams. In the real world, what may happen is that a woman or a man may put their ambitions and dreams on hold because they feel obligated to perform other tasks which are more pressing, such as bringing up children. A man who insists on having kids before a woman is ready for it is crossing this line. If a man decides to take a job in another state and does not consult his wife, then he is crossing a boundary because he is assuming that she will agree with his choices.

As far as spiritual needs go, one may have deeper needs than the other, though should respect those needs. For example, a wife may feel the need to stay close to God, while her husband sees this as illogical. He should, however, appreciate that her need is important and should be met, though she should not insist upon him crossing the line of acceptability and following her view simply because it's important to her.

All of these areas are vitally important if a relationship is to grow and flourish. Mutual understanding, mutual support and mutual agreement that each can follow their own agenda is vital though the picture gets complex when there are children involved. For example, the wife's needs may not be met because she has an obligation to the children. The husband's needs may not be met because he has an obligation to work hard to provide for the family. When children are involved, the couple should be sufficiently stable in order to give the kids what they need, but neither wife nor husband should have to abandon their hopes and dreams because of the kids. In fact, when they do grab life fully, they actually do give their kids more complete parents who still know how to achieve their hopes and ambitions, regardless of obstacles getting in the way.

Chapter 5 – The Importance of Truth

When a relationship is long term as in a marriage, it's important that the couple is always truthful with each other about what they want out of life. What tends to happen in a careless relationship is that truth gets put to one side. He wants his buddies over to watch football and she puts up with it because she sees that other wives do that too. Doing things because you want to do them and doing things because you feel you should are two separate things. You may be denying the truth by allowing things to happen within a marriage that you really don't like. There are ways that couples can compromise. For example, if he is a sports fanatic and she isn't, she could accept his sports evening if there is something of equal importance to her that is permitted on another night.

The trouble is that people tend to be dishonest about what they really want out of a relationship, and thus bad habits creep into the relationship that skew the boundaries. Perhaps she is too afraid to lose him if she voices her opinion. Perhaps he is too afraid to lose her if he lets her know his inner thoughts or his sexual desires. Instead of doing that, each look for solace in other friendships and the couples become distant as a result of their own lack of honesty.

Truth is often hard to deal with. Sometimes, you want to say something to your partner but put it off because the right moment never seems to come along. The problem with this is that you build up resentment if you can't get your truth across. This can lead to a relationship being very difficult indeed and you may need to set aside a time when you know that your partner is able to listen and give you the attention you desire.

For example, you may have been brooding over something that was said or something that was done and have not given yourself an opportunity to address it. Providing that it involves both of you and is not merely a criticism of your partner, choose a time when your partner is more receptive and remember to talk things through very calmly. It doesn't do anyone any good if you blurt out your truth in an emotional way because when you do that, you do it with the expectation that your partner will instantly understand. They are far more likely to understand if you are calm and can show them that you feel your boundaries have been violated in some way. Your partner wants what is best for you as a couple, and will be open to listening if you approach your truth in this manner.

Similarly, remember to listen to their truths. Perhaps something that you have done has given your partner reason for concern. Let your partner voice his opinion without getting too angry about it. Couples make the mistake of not allowing each other to be truthful for fear of reprisal. When you are in a loving relationship, you should be able to talk things through and come to conclusions that are good for both of you.

Distance

The boundary of distance is a very useful tool to use if you find that your emotions are too raw. Distancing yourself from your partner and calming down will help you considerably to view any problems that you may have from a reasonable distance, rather than letting emotions rule what you say. Remember, you cannot take something back once you have said it, and the hurried words which hurt your partner could do damage to the relationship which may be hard to repair. It is far wiser to distance yourself until you have a clearer picture of the situation and are able to tackle it in a much calmer way.

Often the truth that you shout out in anger is not actually the truth that you feel in your heart.

Words can be said which exaggerate the situation and you may not be able to take those words back at a later time. Another thing to avoid is bringing up the same thing time and time again when an argument starts. It is frustrating for a partner to be continually criticized and it's far better to distance yourself and to work out solutions that you think may work for both of you.

Truth always wins the day, but truth needs to have its time and needs to be within the boundaries of decency. For example, if a man disappoints his wife in bed, it's not a time for her to tell him his performance is bad. The limits of decency would mean that she would get better results if instead of criticizing, she encouraged him to be more adventurous. Similarly, a woman won't take kindly to a man telling her she has hairs on her chin. However, she will respond favorably if he buys her a hair removal system for her beauty because he heard that it's quite good. The two examples shown here show that truth can be helpful, but that you do need to be aware of feelings when using truth as if you cross the boundary of understanding and empathizing, truth won't help the relationship.

However, truth used to help trust to grow is very beneficial indeed, and a relationship built on that kind of foundation is very strong and can last through bad times and good.

Chapter 6 – Consequences of Crossing Boundaries

When boundaries are crossed, no matter how unintentional, there have to be consequences. A woman who is beaten by her husband will know that she fears him more than trusts him. The consequences of his actions are therefore that they have a negative impact on the relationship. Similarly, if a married person crosses the boundary that should be placed between him/her and temptation to unfaithfulness, the consequence could be the loss of the marriage. Thus it can be seen that boundaries even between married people and outsiders are vital to the way in which a marriage progresses. Society places these boundaries that married people should not cross as a high priority. For example, a woman should not have an affair outside of her marriage. A man should not be unfaithful either, and if this boundary is crossed, unfortunately, it's unlikely to be forgiven.

The consequences of crossing boundaries can be:

- Lack of trust

- Lack of respect

- Lack of confidence

Each of these is important to marriage. An example can be given here of when a man crosses an emotional boundary and mocks something that his wife feels self-conscious about. She will lose her trust in him emotionally because she knows that he has stooped low enough to hurt her in that way. When boundaries are crossed, one of the consequences that is the most serious threat to marriage is lack of respect. Respect is the cornerstone of any relationship and this should be a two-way thing in a marriage.

The reason for pointing out the consequences is so that married people can see clearly what happens when boundaries are crossed and why they are so vital to a marriage. Two individual people have come together with mutual trust and mutual understanding, but when one of them forgets the basis of the relationship and crosses a boundary, the relationship takes on a different perspective. It becomes one of suspicion, resentment and perhaps mistrust.

There are actions that people can take as a consequence of boundaries being crossed. For example, if a meal is made for a set time and a husband is perpetually late for the meal, it would be reasonable for the family to start eating dinner without the husband and for the wife to put his meal into the microwave to be heated up later. This is the consequence in a setting that is quite common. The woman, having cooked the meal at the agreed time, feels disappointment when her husband does not respect her work and fails to turn up on time over and over again. When faced with the choice between having a meal on time with his family and heating up a meal in the microwave, chances are that the lesson learned would mean he would apologize and make more effort in future.

Abusive conversations within a relationship fall outside of acceptable boundaries. The consequences could be that the person receiving the abuse would be quite within their rights to leave the room and not to return until the abuse has finished. The action should tell the abuser that his abusive talk is not being listened to and powerless in his efforts to get his message across, he should learn to be more thoughtful toward his partner.

In the case of an overspending wife, a man would be perfectly within his rights to stop her credit card until such a time as she has learned accountability, or can earn money herself to spend on the things that she wants.

As can be seen in all of these cases, there are consequences and these help to put the relationship back on course again, if they are employed and kept to. Once one person backs down, the whole chain of events acts like dominoes in a chain, one tumbling after the other, until the situation is out of control. Rather than letting this happen, taking appropriate action at the time when a boundary is crossed is much more sensible.

Chapter 7 – Sexual Boundaries In Marriage

One area where boundaries may be necessary – even required – is in the bedroom. Sex is different things to different people at different stages of their lives. In the early days of courtship and marriage, it's likely that you just can't get enough of one another. And because the relationship is new, you may not be 100% honest about your own sexual preferences or desires, because it's a difficult subject to talk about – especially outside the bedroom. However, it's something you really need to address with your partner, because sex is going to be a big part of your marriage for the foreseeable future, and if you don't get the balance right, your marriage may not survive.

People who say sex is not important in marriage are either lying, not interested, or at least 85, because sex is important – so important that if the sex is wrong, it impacts on other areas of your life and your marriage. Humans are the only species that engage in sex for purposes other than reproduction, and that's where the problems begin. If you're just making babies, you have a logical and identifiable agenda, but when fun gets into the equation, it's not always fun, is it?

Sometimes, you have to wonder if the way we talk openly about sexuality, desires, fantasies and other stuff is really an improvement on the days when any mention of anything 'downstairs' was strictly taboo. They say a little knowledge is a dangerous thing, and it possibly is, because back in the day, nobody knew what their friends were getting – or not getting – and therefore they had no reason to be discontented. And it just wasn't done to talk about 'that sort of thing.'

Realistically, it is good to talk – about everything, and particularly about sex. The problem is, although everyone seems to be talking about sex, husbands and wives often don't talk about it to each other, and they really should. There are all sorts of reasons they don't talk about it – they're worried that if they open up and reveal their fantasies, their partner will go off them. And they're just as worried that if their partners reveal their fantasies, they won't be able to live up to them, or that they will regard them in a different, less favorable light.

Expectations are artificially raised by the wide

availability of pornography. Real men don't have huge penises – at least, most of them don't. And real women don't have perfect bodies and perfect make up, even in the throes of passion. Make that especially in the throes of passion. So, what can a married couple do to address these potential problems? They can set sexual boundaries within their marriage, that's what.

In order to do this, they have to be candid, understanding and respectful, so that they can talk about their sexual expectations and fears without fear of resentment or ridicule. That can be a difficult balance to achieve, because matters sexual are usually charged with emotion and the fear of failure. He may feel he is not satisfying her, and she may feel he no longer finds her attractive.

The key to setting sexual boundaries is to recognize what you are comfortable with, and what you find disturbing or a turn off. Until you establish that, you really can't set realistic, manageable boundaries within your marriage.

When?

If your man wants sex first thing in the morning, but you prefer closeness before you go to sleep, there's a boundary in the making, because nobody – whether married, in a relationship or just dating casually – should ever have sex just to please someone else. It should be a shared, mutual pleasure, because it's a participating sport for two players, and the best matches happen when both parties are committed to the game.

So, how would you set this boundary? Certainly not by saying, 'Why don't you ever want sex when I'm in the mood? Why does it always have to be when you want it?' All that's going to do is put him on the defensive, and likely lead to an argument. That sort of statement immediately puts the other partner in the wrong, and it's not wrong for him to want sex in the morning, any more than it's wrong for you to prefer sex at night – or vice versa, as the case may be. Unless you communicate what you want, he's not going to know how you feel. That sounds like a no-brainer, but it's surprising how much resentment builds up in marriages because one partner expects the other to know what they want – or more usually don't want.

So, any attempt to set a boundary has to start with an explanation of your feelings, that isn't couched in condemnatory terms. Maybe you could start by saying something like, 'I love it when we make love, because you're such a good lover, and you know what turns me on.' If that compliment doesn't get his full attention, then he doesn't deserve you, because everyone – guys and girls alike – likes to be told they're hot in bed. Then you can move on to say, 'I'd enjoy it even more if we could make love in the evenings more often. I'm not a morning person, and I think it would be so hot if we made out at night. What do you think?'

You're not apportioning any sort of blame here, just stating facts in a teasing kind of way – you're saying you could both have a lot more fun simply by rescheduling your lovemaking. Now the door is open for him to communicate his feelings. Maybe he feels too tired for sex at night – or perhaps he thinks you do. Anyway, now you've opened up dialogue, so you can both discuss your feelings, and maybe come to a compromise if you need to. At least you're communicating, and you can now work on setting that boundary so you make love when you both want to. The bonus is, the sex will be more enjoyable for both of you.

If your husband is not prepared to compromise on this, he's demonstrating a clear and unacceptable lack of respect for your feelings, as well as exercising certain amount of control. He wants to say when you will have sex – because it isn't making love it you are not both in the mood at the same time. He's crossing a boundary that is totally unacceptable, and in that case, the only way you can bring him around to the idea of compromise is to refuse him. If you go along with his demands – and they are demands, if he's not respecting your wishes in this – then you are sending the message that it's okay for him to have sex whenever he wants, regardless of what you want. After a few refusals, he should be ready to talk again, and if he doesn't, maybe you need to examine your marriage and determine if there are other areas where he disregards your wishes.

Dirty talk

Just as important as when you make love is what you do when you go to bed. Again, this can be an area fraught with difficulties, and it can be difficult to get a dialogue going. One of the things that most guys love but many girls have problems with is dirty talk. For guys, it's a big turn on, but some girls feel like sluts if they talk dirty, and that's not conducive to a great sexual experience. So, you need to get that across, in a non-judgmental way. Start by saying that you want to please him, and do stuff that turns him on, but you're just not comfortable with the idea of talking dirty, because it's not something you have experience of.

Don't say you can't understand why he wants you to do such a thing, because that's negative and confrontational, and it won't help anyone. He's not wrong for wanting you to talk dirty, and you're not wrong for not wanting to oblige. Again it's a case of different strokes for different folks, and you need to at least try to understand where he's coming from. Read some articles, and watch some videos on YouTube to get an idea of what's entailed in dirty talk and why your man enjoys it.

The first thing you'll find out is that dirty talk doesn't mean screaming crude words at the top of your voice. Maybe it's time for a new perspective – or even a new term for dirty talk, because the current one is just so misleading it isn't true. Dirty talk isn't always about what you say, it's more about how you say it. If you can whisper in his ear, sort of breathlessly, it's not about what you say. He'll pick up that you are excited and looking forward to making love, and it will get him excited too.

Maybe you can talk about what you want him to do to you, or what you want to do to him. Tell him about your fantasies – anything you can think of, but keep it on topic and related to sex. And sound as if you mean it, otherwise it won't work.

If, after reading up about dirty talk, you still don't feel able to indulge in it, then you need to set that boundary. Tell your man you just don't feel comfortable with it, and although you want to please him, you really can't do it in that way. If he's a loving, understanding man, he'll realize that, and he won't push you on the subject. However, it he tries to talk you into talking dirty – or anything else you don't feel comfortable with – then you have to convey to him that you won't be coerced into anything just because he wants to try it. Lovemaking is all about mutual pleasure, and if one of you is doing something against their will, then that element of mutual pleasure is missing, and the lovemaking will not be as enjoyable as it should be.

Role play

Often, couples engage in role play to spice up their love life. Several scenarios are possible – doctor or nurse and patient, prostitute and client, submissive and domination, teacher and pupil, strangers meeting and having sex, porn stars – the possibilities are only limited by your imagination. Role play allows a couple to shed their identities, and with it, the constraints and inhibitions of everyday life. For a short time, they can be someone else, and take their lovemaking to a new, exciting level.

Role play is harmless, and it can be great fun. However, if one of the partners can only ever enjoy sex through role play, and insists on it every time, maybe you need to set a boundary. Living a fantasy is fun, but when the fantasy becomes more important than real life, you have to pause and ask why that should be. What is lacking in your relationship that your partner can only enjoy sex as role play? It's bound to make the other partner feel inadequate and even unloved, so it needs to be talked through calmly, without drama or animosity.

Why does he – or she – need the buzz of being someone else in order to enjoy sex? It places an unreasonable burden on the other partner, because effectively it means they cannot be themselves and act naturally during this most natural and intimate of acts. Fantasy becomes more important than reality, and the other partner has a right to know why this is so.

Maybe one partner is watching too much porn, and has lost touch with the reality of making love in an intimate setting with someone they truly love. Another possibility is that the partner who is hooked on fantasies wishes their partner was different in some way. Either of these possibilities is unhealthy, and has no place in a happy marriage of equal partners. Don't be coerced into acting out your partner's fantasies – tell them that this is a boundary you will not cross, because it effectively invalidates your life together. And encourage your partner to talk about why they always feel the need to act out fantasies during sex. If he or she cannot open up to you, maybe they need to talk to a counsellor – either alone or as a couple.

A healthy sexual relationship is an integral part of a happy marriage. However, each partner needs to understand what is acceptable and what is not, whether it is in the things they expect you to do, or the timing and frequency of your lovemaking. Remember this should be a shared pleasure, so both partners should be happy with what takes place in the bedroom.

It is therefore perfectly fine to set sexual boundaries, and to discuss those boundaries with your partner outside the bedroom. Nobody – man or woman – should ever be coerced into doing something they are uncomfortable with, or doing something they find disturbing or a turn off. Each partner has the right to have their wishes – and their body – respected, and setting sexual boundaries will help to ensure that this happens, and that both partners enjoy and look forward to making love together.

Chapter 8: Setting Boundaries For Controlling Behavior

Marriage is a partnership. That might sound obvious, but it's surprising how many husbands and wives want to control every aspect of their partner's behavior. This is clearly crossing a boundary, since no person should ever control the behavior of another.

Adults are hopefully responsible enough to make their own decisions as to what they wear, whom they make friends with, what they eat and drink, and how they live their lives. However, if your husband or wife is dictating these aspects of your life, they are exercising unacceptable influence over you, and it should not be allowed to continue.

This is a difficult one to deal with, because someone who is used to being in control is not going to take kindly to his or her partner kicking back against that control.

Obviously, the best way to deal with this is not to allow the controlling behavior to occur in the first place, but it's not as easy as that. The controller will gain trust by appearing to advise at first, and then ramp it up to the stage where if you don't take their 'advice,' they are not happy, and will cause an argument.

Often, this sort of behavior stems from insecurity, or a wish to create a perfect partner. Whatever the reason, the controlling partner is crossing a boundary that really should not be crossed.

Controlling your appearance

Maybe your husband doesn't let you go out alone, or if he does, he wants to decide what you wear, and whether you wear make-up or not. He may say, 'Why do you have to wear make-up when you are going out without me? You must be looking to attract another man,' and no amount of reassurance will convince him that you are not getting made up for any other reason than that it makes you feel good when you know your best.

Similarly, he'll say, 'You're not going out in that are you? It makes you look fat/old/like a whore.' If you know that none of these things are true, and you are happy with the way you look, you should not give in to these demands and change your clothes or remove your make-up. He's not really hoping that you will change or remove your make-up – if you do, he will still not be happy. He doesn't want you to go out at all, and he's hoping that if he makes enough fuss, you'll decide that it isn't worth the hassle and stay in.

Of course, you may well feel like that, but you should go out anyway. Just say calmly that you are not looking to meet anyone else, you just want to enjoy time with friends or family. And refuse to make any changes to your appearance. Try not to be drawn into an argument either, because that will just ruin your outing. If you can do this a few times, he may desist in his behavior when he sees that it's having no effect. However, if he doesn't, you need to talk calmly about it when you are both happy and relaxed. Reassure him that there is no hidden agenda, but that sometimes it's nice to go out with friends or family, and when you do, you want to look and feel good, so you make an effort with your appearance.

If he cannot accept this, and you have given him no reason to mistrust you, maybe you need to talk to a couple's counselor to determine why he feels the need to control you in this way. Maybe a previous partner did go out alone, and eventually met someone else and cheated on him, but you cannot be responsible for her decisions, and nor should you be made to pay for them by submitting to controlling behavior. You need to make this clear, either alone or with help from a counselor or therapist.

Another reason your partner may wish to control how you look is that he has a pre-formed idea of his ideal partner – the way she looks, dresses and behaves. This can be more difficult to deal with, because he's not likely to be open to a convincing argument. Of course, nobody should ever try to change another person to fit his or her own blueprint of the ideal partner. This is another example of unacceptable stepping over boundaries.

Partners are attracted to one another because of something unique in their character and appearance that strikes a chord in someone else and makes them want to spend their life with that person. If one partner tries to change the other, having gone into the relationship with open eyes, they are also crossing a boundary in a totally unacceptable way. Everyone has the right to be their own person, regardless of the expectations of others.

If your partner cannot accept and celebrate your individuality, then maybe he or she is not the right person for you. Someone like that will not be satisfied until you are a clone of their ideal man or woman. And if you go along with it, you will not be satisfied, because you will no longer be your own person – you will be someone else's ideal, and that may be nothing like the real you.

Controlling your associations with friends and family

Another way in which a controlling partner may try to influence your life is by controlling who you spend time with, and also influencing the amount of time you spend with them. This can happen for a number of reasons. If your partner has never enjoyed a close family relationship, he or she may not understand why you want to spend a lot of time with your parents, siblings or cousins. Or your partner may not feel welcome or comfortable around them.

This is not your problem – and your partner should not try to limit the time you spend with them, as long as it's within reason. For example, if you insist on spending every evening with your parents, or having them visit every day, that's not fair to your own husband or wife and family. You need time together as a family unit, and if you don't facilitate that, then you are overstepping a boundary, because effectively you are putting your relatives before your own partner and family.

However, assuming that the amount of time you spend with your family is within reason, and you are not following their wishes at the expense of your partner's expectations from your relationship, what can you do about this type of controlling behavior? It's a tricky one, because whatever you do or day, your partner will accuse you – rightly or wrongly – of putting your family before your relationship.

Again, you need to be firm but calm, and explain that, although you love your partner, you also love your family and friends in a different way, and you want to spend time with them. Your family – and possibly most of your friends – were in your life before you met your husband and wife, and their influence and your interactions with them helped to make you the person your partner fell in love with. Therefore it is unreasonable for your partner to expect you to limit or cut off contact with them. If your partner doesn't want to spend time with your friends and family, you shouldn't insist that they do, and by the same token, they shouldn't discourage you from spending time with the people you love.

Controlling the finances

Money can be a big cause of discontent in relationships. Each partner has their own ideas of what constitutes reasonable expenditure, and very often these ideas will clash. One partner may consider it to be perfectly fine to spend a few hundred bucks a month on eating out and going to the theatre, while the other partner may prefer to spend disposable income on stuff for the house or clothes, because they want to see something for their money, and a meal or a show is a transient pleasure, however good it might be.

Generally, couples discuss budgeting and casual expenditure, and arrive at a solution that suits both parties, but sometimes, one partner can be excessively controlling of the marital finances. Usually, this is the husband, but it can also be true of the wife. It may be that the husband feels that, if his wife does not go out to work and earn money, she should have no say in how the income is spent. This is a very outdated view of things, and doesn't take into account the wife's valuable contribution of setting up and maintaining a home, raising children, and preparing meals for the family.

If your partner is controlling the finances, and you do not have reasonable access to money for shopping, or you have to account for every penny you spend, then your partner is overstepping a fundamental boundary, and you have every right to ask for your fair share of the family finances. By controlling your access to money, your partner is controlling more than just one aspect of your life. Marriage is a partnership, and it should be an equal partnership, but if one partner is controlling the funds, you are being denied access to and responsibility for decision-making in the matter of family finances.

It can be difficult to get around this problem,

because someone who is used to controlling the finances is not likely to relinquish that control easily or willingly. You need to point out that, as an equal partner in the marriage, you expect to be involved in budgeting and financial decision making, and that you feel it shows a lack of respect and trust in your judgment to deny this.

The thing is, if you don't at least try to mitigate any form of controlling behaviour, you are effectively condoning it, and it will appear to your partner that his or her control is justified. Controlling behaviour in what should be an equal partnership should never be tolerated or validated, and you owe it to yourself to do everything you can to break the cycle and remove the control from your marriage.

Chapter 9: The Boundaries of Friendship in Marriage

No matter how much you and your spouse love each other and want to be with each other, no man or woman is an island, and you both need other people in your lives. You cannot possibly supply all each other's needs for companionship, conversation and intellectual stimulation, and nor should you try. Each of you should cultivate friendships with people who share your interests and beliefs, both men and women. It's also advisable to have some friends who are 'opposite' in a number of ways, to keep life interesting for everyone concerned.

Some friends will have been with you since your single days, and shared the ups and downs of your life, providing help, support, or even just a shoulder to cry on when you need it. These friends will probably know you almost as well as you know yourself, or even better. Other friends will come into your life through work, the school run, your children, and your leisure activities. Some of these friends will be really important in your life, others will just be there when you want to have fun and hang out. All of them have the potential to enrich your lives, singly and as a couple. And all of them also have the potential to cause problems within the marriage, so you need to decide how friendships fit into the framework of your marriage, what boundaries are necessary, and how you can enjoy your friendships without upsetting or neglecting your partner, or putting your marriage in jeopardy.

Your partner should be your best friend

It goes without saying that your husband or wife should be your best friend, and that no other friend should ever take his or her place as your number one go-to confidant. If any of your friends try to take your partner's place, or if you come to regard them as more important in your life than your spouse, you really need to rethink both relationships.

Yes, it's sometimes easier to talk about some things to a close friend than your partner – particularly 'women's things.' However, if a time comes when you confide things to your friends that you keep secret from your partner, or if you ask them not to discuss the things you've talked about with anyone else, it's a sign that something is seriously wrong somewhere. It may be a problem in your marriage, or it may be that you are prioritizing friendships ahead of your relationship. Either way, it's something that needs to be addressed.

Friends and partners provide different forms of support, and you may find that you can discuss things easily with your friend but you find it difficult or embarrassing to discuss the same things with your partner. That's different to not being able or willing to discuss stuff with your partner. If that's the case, and you're keeping secrets, then you've overstepped a fundamental boundary in marriage.

Boundaries also need to be set with friends – especially friends of the opposite sex. It is not appropriate for your friend to call at midnight, or spend all day texting or messaging you. And it's not appropriate to keep your meetings and conversations secret from your spouse. If you have a separate, secret email account and/or social media account that your partner knows nothing about, it's absolutely not appropriate, and cannot be justified.

The thing is, if you see the need to keep your activities and communications secret from your spouse, then they cannot really be described as innocent. There may be no sort of sexual feelings attached to your interaction with your friend, but if he or she is party to events that are happening in your marriage, or problems you are having, and if your partner doesn't know that you've shared this information, a boundary has been transgressed.

This sort of confiding in someone you are not in a relationship with is likely to build up and emotional attachment between the two of you that is even stronger than the bond with your spouse. You don't have to be physically unfaithful and exchange bodily fluids to cheat on your partner. In fact, emotional infidelity is often regarded as a worse betrayal than committing adultery, because you have formed a connection at a much deeper level. That sort of intimacy should be the exclusive preserve of your partner.

The best type of friend of either sex will realize that and will never try to come between you, and those are the types of friendship you want to cultivate, because they can be a valuable support when things go wrong in your life.

The balance between friends and partners can be a tricky one to preserve, but it's well worth aiming for, because both you and your spouse can get a lot from a healthy friendship. It gives you another dimension, a person to care about in a different way, and someone else to share areas of your life with. And that's the clue – friends should be a healthy part of your life, but your life should not revolve around them, any more than their lives should revolve around you. Keep it real, and there should be no negative impact on our marriage, because the acceptable boundaries will be maintained.

When your partner and your friend don't get on

Not everyone can get along together all the time. People are individuals, and there are bound to be personality clashes, especially over a number of years. The people you choose as friends may not necessarily be your partner's first choice of leisure companion and confidant, but you should each make an effort to get on with each other's friends. After all, your partner is a person of good taste and intelligent discrimination – and if they are not, why are you spending your life with them anyway?

As a decent person, your partner recognized something good in their friends, and decided they wanted to get to know them better, and share areas of their life with them. Even if you can't see what your partner sees in one or more of his or her friends, you should at least respect their judgement, and try to find something to like about their friend.

Even if you can't, you owe it to your partner to at least get along with their friends, unless there is obviously something unhealthy about the friendship. For example, if the friend is dishonest, or even criminally inclined, and is attempting to draw your partner into illegal activity, it is perfectly reasonable to hope that your partner will end the friendship, and even encourage them to do so. After all, involvement in criminal acts is eventually going to have a negative and potentially devastating impact on your relationship. And if you have children, you really don't want such negative influences in their lives.

This is an extreme example of an instance when you may be justified in asking your partner to end a friendship, but they are few and far between. In normal circumstances, it would be a totally unacceptable transgression of a boundary within your marriage to insist that your partner ended a friendship if he or she is not willing to do so, and there is no good reason why they should, other than your dislike of the friend.

Responsible adults have the right to choose their own friends, and for their choices to be accepted by the people close to them. If you really can't tolerate your spouse's friend, or if the situation is reversed, the constructive thing to do is to keep the friend and the spouse apart as much as possible. There's no point in forcing a get together if at least one of the parties is uncomfortable with it. Arrange to meet your friend away from the family home, or when your partner is otherwise engaged, and then you can relax and enjoy quality time with your friend, knowing that you are not annoying or upsetting your spouse. And suggest that they do the same if you have a disliking for a particular friend.

This is the adult way to deal with the issue of friends who are potential cuckoos in the nest. Friendships are valuable, and it is unreasonable to expect your partner to give up on a good friend for no better reason than that you don't like them. Equally, it is unreasonable to insist that a friend is always welcome in your home when this clearly isn't the case. It's unfair to the friend, and it's unfair to the spouse who has the issue with the friend.

With negotiation, love and acceptance, it is possible for both partners to enjoy healthy and fulfilling friendships with people their partners are not comfortable with. Like all aspects of married life, it just needs a little work and some compromising along the way to keep everyone happy and fulfilled.

Chapter 10: The Boundaries of Social Media and Life Sharing

These days, pretty much everyone has at least one social media account, whatever their age and lifestyle. It can be a great way to keep in touch with friends and family – especially these days, when many families live in different parts of the country, or even the world, due to the need to earn a living or enjoy a better quality of life. Social media is great for networking too, both personally and professionally. However, it has its limitations, and there are boundaries that should not be overstepped if you want to keep your marriage happy and your dignity intact.

Why Facebook can be bad for your marriage

One thing neither of you should do is play out your most intimate moments in Facebook statuses. The problems you are having – or the great sex you're having for that matter – are your business and your business alone. The thing with

Facebook is too many people have an opinion on anything and everything, whether they are qualified to deliver it or not. If you really need to talk to a stranger about your marriage difficulties, make that person a qualified relationships counsellor rather than a Facebook friend.

It's no exaggeration to say that the power of social media has been responsible for breaking up relationships, mainly because the people who respond to statuses often tend to see things in black and white. They have one side of the story, and that's what they base their judgements on. There are always two sides to every tale of woe, and both sides deserve an equal, unbiased hearing. That is never going to happen on Facebook, no matter who is on your friends list.

The brutal truth is that most of the people who are going to see your dramatic relationship statuses on Facebook are not actually interested in the state of your marriage, or in your feelings about it. They're interested in the drama, and want to be involved in it. And the best way to get involved in it is to make comments and offer 'advice' that gets them noticed. They don't really care about you, because if they did, they'd be contacting you privately to offer support and advice, away from the public glare of social media.

The problem is, when you are unhappy, you tend to clutch at any straws to make the pain go away, and because the internet is fairly anonymous in many ways, it seems an easy option to air your grievances there and ask for advice and support. What you should really be doing is talking to your partner and trying to resolve your difficulties, or if that isn't possible, confiding in a trusted friend or family member.

Facebook can give an entirely false sense of proportion at times. It can seem that everyone is in a happy relationship and having a good time, except for you, when nothing could be further from the truth. People tend to post the highlights of their life on social media, because they want other people to see just how good their lives are. They don't post the mundane, or the stuff that goes wrong, so what you get is an edited highlights version of the lives of your friends, rather than the real deal.

Their lives are no better or worse than your own, but it seems as if that is the case, and it can foster a false sense of resentment towards your own life and your partner. It can seem that he is the only man in the civilized world that doesn't organize a lovely surprise for his spouse every weekend, or she is the only woman who doesn't put a delicious, healthy, home cooked meal on the table every night – and it's all an illusion.

So, as well as not broadcasting your own discontent on social media, you should make a conscious effort not to read too much into the seemingly perfect lives of others. Unless you are following the statuses of media celebrities, the lives of your Facebook friends will be very similar to your own, so don't allow Facebook to come between you and your spouse, and don't use it as a way of taking public revenge on him or her for imagined or actual transgressions.

Respecting your partner's privacy on social media

While social media is by definition a public platform – the clue is in the name – it's also an area where privacy needs to be respected by both partners. You should each have separate accounts, and separate log in details which are not shared with your partner. Social media used correctly can be diverting, entertaining and useful, but you need to be free to do your own thing, and be your own person.

For some reason, some couples seem to think it's a good idea to share a social media account. While togetherness is always a good thing, sometimes it can be taken too far, and sharing a Facebook account is a good example of this. What if you post something your spouse does not agree with? Or take offence at something that's said? When the account is shared, two viewpoints are also being shared, and they may not always be concurrent and coinciding.

If a spouse insists on either sharing a social media account or having unlimited access to their partner's account, they are overstepping the fundamental boundaries of privacy and trust in the marriage. Everyone is entitled to their own space, where they can be who they want to be, and decide whether or not to share access to that space with anyone else. It may well be that your husband or wife shares all the details of their social media account, but it must be their decision, freely made, otherwise resentment is inevitable.

When online friendships overstep the boundaries

Social media is a place where connections and friendships are made all over the world, with people of different backgrounds, ages and interests. These online friendships can be every bit as valid and valuable as 'real life' friendships, but they can also get very intense, very quickly – especially if one or both of the parties to the friendship is going through difficulties in their private life.

When does an online friendship overstep the boundaries of trust and appropriate behavior in a marriage? It can be difficult to know until it is too late, because what starts as friendly Banter with maybe a little flirting can quickly accelerate into emotional infidelity before you realize it. If you look on an online friend as more important to you and more exciting and interesting than your spouse, then a boundary has been crossed, and the only thing to do if you are serious about maintaining the integrity of the marriage is to end the friendship. If you are reluctant to do that, then you have to decide which is more important – your marriage or your online friendship.

If you are spending more time communicating with online friends than your spouse, you need to ask yourself why this should be. What is the online friend providing that is lacking in your marriage? Is it intelligent and interesting conversation, attention, appreciation, a sexual frisson, or something else? Maybe it is more than one of these vital ingredients for intimacy between a couple. If you can identify the missing ingredient, you can perhaps recover the relationship with your spouse if you really want to do that.

However, before you can do that, you need to end the online friendship, no matter how reluctant you are to do that. Once a friend becomes more important than your life partner, you need to modify the friendship or end it, and if it's an online friendship, the only way is to end it, because there is always going to be the danger that the friendship will again move into inappropriate territory.

If you suspect your partner is involved in an inappropriate online friendship, you need to discuss your concerns calmly, without getting involved in an argument or recriminations. It may well be that your partner doesn't realize that he or she is spending too much time with an online friend at the expense of their relationship, but when you point out that you are worried about their level of attachment, they should be able to reassure you unhesitatingly.

If they cannot, you may have real cause for concern, but you should try not to offer an ultimatum along the lines of 'End this friendship, or it's the end of our marriage,' because that will merely put your partner on the defensive, and they will refuse to accede to your request. Then what are you going to do? If you follow through with your threat to end the marriage, you may be giving up on something that is worthy of being saved. And if you don't follow through with it, and allow things to continue as they are, then your partner will think it's okay to carry on with an inappropriate friendship, or any other challenging behaviour, because although you make a lot of noise, you don't actually carry out your threats.

Ultimatums rarely serve any useful, positive purpose. If they are carried through, they can cause resentment between the partners in the marriage, and if they are seen to be empty threats, they can engender a lack of respect, which has no place in a healthy marriage. There is always an alternative to an ultimatum, and in fact it's a lazy way to communicate, because it slams the door on negotiation, and negotiation can be a valuable and effective resource when two partners have fundamental differences of opinion to settle.

Social media can be a fun resource, as well as a useful tool for networking and catching up with people you have lost touch with over the years. However, it can also wreck relationships, so you need to have some boundaries in place within your marriage to ensure that Facebook and your online friends do not drive a wedge between you and cause problems within your marriage. Treat social media as the useful resource it is, rather than a substitute for communication and intimacy between you and your partner.

Chapter 11: Boundaries of Fidelity in Marriage

In some circles, it's considered to be old fashioned these days to be faithful to your partner, both emotionally and physically. There's a school of thought that says staying with the same partner for decades and remaining totally faithful is an unrealistic expectation. However, if this is the way you are thinking, you have to ask yourself why you entered into marriage in the first place. The whole point of making a public declaration of love and honour for another person is to show the world that you freely commit to one another. If you are not going to do that, there seems no point in getting married – unless you love dressing up, speeches and wedding cake.

For people who are committed to maintaining fidelity in their marriage, the task is not going to be easy. Just because there is a wedding ring on your finger, it doesn't mean you are immune to the attractions of the opposite sex, and there will be times when your resolve to be faithful is tested. Your partner will face the same tests, and how you deal with them is crucial to the continuing strength and success of your shared relationship.

The boundaries of fidelity in your marriage are probably the most important of all, because from them stem truth, honesty and respect. You need to decide together what constitutes fidelity. Too many people assume that infidelity is purely physical, but it's not so easy or so clear cut as that. Yes, physical infidelity can be hurtful, but there is a difference between a physical affair and an emotional affair, which may or may not eventually become physical.

When a husband or wife has sex with another person outside the marriage, it may be a purely physical act, or there may be more to it than that. If it's purely physical, it is possible for the marriage to recover, because anyone can make a mistake, and if they are truly repentant and promise to amend their behaviour, maybe they deserve forgiveness, and a chance to show how truly sorry they are and how much they value their marriage.

However, if an emotional connection has formed, that is something different. People can be overwhelmed and carried away by physical feelings, especially in certain circumstances.

Maybe the people concerned have been drinking, and their inhibitions are down as a result, or maybe it's just a 'feel good moment' that gets out of hand. Emotional connections don't happen like that though – they build up gradually over time, because the people concerned allow it to happen. This goes further than mere friendship, and it is a total betrayal of the trust and intimacy that should be shared between husband and wife.

A lot of hurt and misunderstanding can be avoided if, as a couple, you take the time to define the boundaries of fidelity at the start of your relationship. You need to be on the same page here – if one partner wants an open marriage, while the other expects fidelity, there is going to be great unhappiness at some point, and that point will probably come sooner rather than later.

It is unreasonable on a number of levels for either partner to insist on no contact or interaction with the opposite sex. For a start, this sounds a clear signal to the partner that you do not trust their behaviour in potentially challenging situations, and therefore feel the need to impose stringent behavioural restrictions. Not only does this demonstrate a complete lack of trust in the other partner, it also shows a lack of respect for their judgement and integrity. You must allow your partner to demonstrate that they know the difference between right and wrong, and that they can be trusted to make the right decisions in their own right, without the constraints of an unreasonable boundary.

This type of extreme boundary setting worryingly demonstrates a desire for total domination and control of their partner, and is a blatant abuse of the boundary system, which is designed to lay down guidelines for appropriate behaviour and encourage respect for the feelings and beliefs of both partners within the marriage. The right boundaries foster a spirit of love, freedom, accountability and responsibility within the marriage, because both spouses have guidelines within which to work towards a happy, mutually fulfilling relationship.

Arbitrary boundary setting such as strictly limiting or forbidding interaction with members of the opposite sex goes against that spirit of love and freedom and is bound to cause resentment and bitterness. The partner who is subjected to such restrictions will feel untrusted and unloved, and that is not a good foundation for any relationship, let alone marriage.

It is preferable to decide jointly what, if any, restrictions are placed on your spouse's dealings with the opposite sex. For instance, are you comfortable with your partner spending time alone with someone else? If so, how much is reasonable? What about contact via emails, texts or phone calls? How much contact is too much?

As a rule of thumb, if your partner's relationship with another person is taking priority over your joint relationship, a boundary has been crossed. If you prefer someone else's company to your partner's, and will cancel arrangements with your partner in order to spend time with that person, then you are into the realms of emotional infidelity. That may or may not develop into physical infidelity, but in any case, the relationship has progressed beyond the bounds of appropriateness and the situation needs to be addressed if the marriage is to survive intact.

It is not helpful to blame the unfaithful partner totally for their transgressions, and you have to accept some responsibility yourself. In very rare cases, the fault for infidelity may lie with one partner, but generally, there are faults on both sides, and you need to discuss frankly and honestly why the infidelity occurred, without apportioning blame to one partner or the other.

The whole point of setting boundaries in marriage is to encourage both spouses to be accountable and take responsibility for their behaviour. Having acknowledged that they have made a mistake and apologised, they must then change their behaviour to bring it back within acceptable, mutually agreed boundaries. If they are unable or unwilling to do that, then the marriage is unlikely to survive in a healthy form, if at all.

When discussing how to move on from infidelity, both partners should try to avoid recriminations, and going over old ground. It's not helpful, and it's a negative way of looking at events. What is needed is a plan for moving forward, and recovering the closeness and intimacy that has been lost. Look to the future, not back to the past. What has happened cannot be changed, but your situation and your future behaviour can be changed, if you so wish.

As part of the boundaries of fidelity, one or both partners may have agreed to forgive one episode of unfaithfulness and move on from it, but they may not be prepared to forgive serial infidelities, and this is perfectly reasonable. Anyone can make a mistake, and behave hurtfully against their partner, but if the same behaviour pattern is repeated, then clearly the unfaithful partner does not see it as unacceptable, or a breach of the boundaries of the marriage. Nor does that partner see a need to change his or her behaviour, even though it may be causing hurt to their spouse.

In this instance, the other partner can be justified in wishing to end the marriage, and if they have previously set this boundary, then they should enforce it. Otherwise the cheating partner will face no pressure to amend the unacceptable behaviour, because there are no consequences of note attached to it. By not enforcing the boundary, the wronged partner is demonstrating a lack of self-esteem, because they deserve a faithful partner, and if they do not have one, then they are perfectly entitled to end the relationship, allow themselves time to heal and then move on with their life. However, some people feel that it is some fault within them that encourages their partner to seek emotional and/or sexual fulfilment with someone else.

In truth, no person can be responsible for the behaviour of another, and not should they shoulder that burden. Setting boundaries in marriage is all about recognising your own responsibility for your conduct within the marriage, and setting up guidelines for that conduct, so that each partner knows what is acceptable, and the likely consequences of transgressing mutually agreed boundaries.

Boundaries in marriage are not about control or apportioning blame. They are about working out a plan of action to live a mutually satisfying and fulfilling life together, based on tolerance, reality, acceptance, compromise and love. Therefore each partner should work towards maintaining those boundaries and, where necessary, changing their behaviour to make the maintenance of those boundaries easier to accomplish.

Conclusion

If you read over the text in this book again, you will see that clearly you are in control of the kind of behavior that you find acceptable to you within your marriage. If this is not the case, then some boundary has been crossed and action needs to be taken to address this. It is easy to lay the blame on the other party, though you do need to assess the whole situation to see what you could do differently to bring a more acceptable response from your loved one. Often, it isn't that they are wrong. It is that the boundaries have never been made clear and they need to be laid out so that there is no misunderstanding in the future.

When you talk to couples about setting boundaries, many respond that they feel that setting them seems very selfish. They argue that going into a marriage with all kinds of rules doesn't feel right. However, what these people are failing to see is that society itself imposes boundaries so that people understand their position in life better and in marriage, it's exactly the same thing. These are levels of acceptability, they are people's expectations within a relationship and it's not unreasonable that people should talk about these in advance of getting married, or bring them up should misunderstandings occur. For example, if a young couple decided that they would marry but that neither one of them wanted children, if one of them crosses the boundary and someday changes their mind, it's likely to cause friction, as the boundary set was one that excluded children.

People have very different expectations in their lives. Setting boundaries before getting married helps to make the air clear between a couple, so that both parties know what to expect of their married life. Thus, a man who expects to be the financial provider should make it clear that he has no wish for his wife to work. To some women, this would be perfectly acceptable, though to a wife who had no idea of this boundary, she may find it shocking that she is being asked to give up a career simply because her husband doesn't want her to work. Thus, you can see that common sense boundaries set up before a marriage takes place help to protect each of the parties against something happening which may ruin the relationship or the respect one party has for the other.

You May Enjoy My Other Books

Author Page

http://hyperurl.co/Jeffdawson

PSYCHOPATH: Manipulation, Con Men And Relationship Fraud

smarturl.it/psychoa

Boundaries: Line Between Right And Wrong

hyperurl.co/boundaries

NARCISSISM: Self Centered Narcissistic Personality Exposed

hyperurl.co/narc

Personality Disorders: Histronic and Borderline Personality Disorders Unmasked

hyperurl.co/borderline

BODY LANGUAGE: How To Spot A Liar And Communicate Clearly

hyperurl.co/bodylang

Tantric Sex and What Women Want - Box Set Collection: Couples Communication and Pleasure Guide

hyperurl.co/sexwomenwant

Boundaries: Crossing The Line: Workplace Success and Office Sex

hyperurl.co/crossline

Personality Disorders: Psychopath or Narcissistic Lover?

hyperurl.co/psy

Boundaries: Parents and Teenagers: Sex, Privacy and Responsibility

hyperurl.co/boundariesteens